N E P A L

© **This edition Roli & Janssen BV 2008**
Third impression
Published in India by
Roli Books in arrangement
with Roli & Janssen BV, the Netherlands
M-75, G. K.-II (Market), New Delhi-110 048, India.
Ph: ++91-11-29212271, 29212782,
Fax: ++91-11-29217185
Email: roli@vsnl.com, Website: rolibooks.com

Published in India by Roli Books
in arrangement with Roli & Janssen BV
M-75 G. K. II Market; New Delhi 110 048, India.
Phone: ++91-11-29212271; Fax: ++91-11-29217185
E-mail: roli@vsnl.com; Website: rolibooks.com

Photo Credits:
Devendra Basnet, Mani Lama, M. Fayolle,
P. Yonzon, Sondeep Shankar, Thomas Kelly

Layout: Naresh L. Mondal, V. Raman

Printed and bound in Singapore

Nepal

MOHIT SATYANAND

Lustre Press
Roli Books

Preceding page 1:
The compassionate eyes of Bodhnath.
Pages 4-5: *The Cholatse Peak in Khumbu, the largely mountainous region of Nepal.*
Pages 6-7: *To the west of Dhaulagiri, lies the valley of Dolpo—the land of the beautiful snow leopard.*
Pages 8-9: *Illuminated with lights and festooned with tiny coloured flags, the Bodhnath temple is worshipped only by Buddhists of Tibetan persuasion.*

A group of monks at prayer, chanting the sacred Buddhist mantras.

Following pages 12-13:
Seen here are the spire-like towers of Kathmandu's crowded Durbar Square, dwarfing the silhouettes of the Malla built temples.

Pages 14-15: *The picturesque Thyangboche monastery in Nepal's eastern Himalayas. Trekkers have to trudge over passes and across many a river to reach this fabled monastery.*

Pages 16-17: *A view of Ganesh Himal from Kathmandu.*

I

IN A WINTER MORNING, the Swayambunath temple rises like a spired island from a sea of mist. Painted on its four sides, the eyes of Buddha watch the vapours thin and the sun rise, to bathe the Kathmandu valley in clear mountain light.

According to a Buddhist legend, in a dim and distant dawn, this verdant valley was supposedly a turquoise lake and home to a celestial lotus, which was a manifestation of the primordial Buddha. Its luminous beauty drew the devout: a million pilgrims who paid obeisance from its grassy shores. Determined to worship from closer, a Chinese pilgrim, Manjushri, breached the valley wall with his sword of wisdom. When the waters drained and the lotus settled, Manjushri built a shrine, which was the foundation of the present day Swayambunath. In Hindu lore, it was Lord Krishna's thunderbolt that cleaved the valley wall and carved the Chobar gorge through which the lake emptied.

In Nepal, Hindu and Buddhist legends are often inseparable, woven into a rich fabric to form the backdrop to a country that is often enigmatic, always exotic. Its monarch is a Harvard alumnus, venerated as an incarnation of the Hindu god Vishnu. But among his subjects, he can count Buddhist lamas, Bon shamans and adherents of the Hindu deviant cult of *Tantra*. In India, *Tantrism* is for the most part extinct, surviving only in stone and wood, in erotica that celebrate the mystery of sexual congress. But in Nepal, the cult has lived on and has influenced the practice of both Buddhism and Hinduism.

Forced by the British to sign a treaty of friendship in that year, the Gorkha kings found their expansionist tendencies checked and their borders frozen. They responded by sealing them. For the next 135 years, the compound of the British resident in Kathmandu housed the only foreigners in Nepal.

The isolation seems an aberration. Throughout its history, Nepal has attracted

missionaries, traders and although less fortuitously, invaders and rulers. The earliest of these belong more to legend than history—the Gopala dynasty installed by Lord Krishna. Later, waves of Tibeto-Burmese settlers probably preceded the earliest documented kings, that is the Kirati dynasty. Claiming origins in the Hindu *Kshatriya* (warrior) caste, this long succession of twenty-five kings ruled Nepal for 800 years, from the fourth century BC to the fourth century AD.

The earliest efforts to popularise Buddhism date back to the Indian emperor Ashoka. An ardent Buddhist proselytizer, he visited Lumbini, the birthplace of Lord Buddha, and raised a column engraved with Buddhist teachings. While it is not clear whether he visited Kathmandu or not, Ashoka did give his daughter, Charumati, in marriage to local royalty. With her husband, Devapala, she founded the cities of Chabahil and Deopatan in the Kathmandu valley.

Meanwhile, the Kiratis yielded to the Licchavis, who like their predecessors claimed to belong to the ruling class of Rajputs in India. Rajputs or not, they introduced the Indian caste system to Nepal and expanded their kingdom both to the east and to the west. In AD 600, the last of the Licchavi rulers, King Vasudeva was succeeded by his son-in-law, Amsuvarman.

King Amsuvarman worked to strengthen ties with India and gave his sister in marriage to Indian nobility. In the north, the Himalayan passes brought to his kingdom the advantages of increased trade between Central and South Asia. It also brought the depredation of a newly unified Tibetan kingdom. To the raider, King Tsrongtsong Gompo, went rich spoils, including Amsuvarman's daughter, Bhrikuti, in marriage.

She took along with her as a sumptuous dowry, her Buddhist faith. Together with the Kings's second wife, a Chinese princess, she converted him, and the rest of Tibet to Buddhism. For their efforts, both Queens passed into Buddhist legend, as the Green Tara and White Tara respectively, still venerated in the *tangkhas* (Buddhist iconic paintings); and most spectacular, is the glowing Green Tara statue at Swayambunath.

Facing page: The Swambunath temple is sacred to both the Hindus and the Buddhists.

During this period, active trade through Nepal brought to it an unprecedented prosperity. Links with China were formalised with the exchange of missions. But till the eighteenth century, Amsuvarman's successors ruled over a valley which was repeatedly troubled by internal strife, foreign incursions and recurrent warfare between Tibet and China, preventing Nepal from developing a stable relationship with her neighbours. Yet, geographical imperatives insured Nepal a continuing importance in north-south trade, and allowed her kings to continue adding to their legacy of religious monuments. Most of this will never be seen.

The Malla dynasties that followed, allowed internecine warring to weaken their empire, rendering the valley and its shrines susceptible to the ravages of Shams-ud-din Ilyas of Bengal. Driven out by widespread Muslim persecution, scores of Indian princes took refuge in Nepal's mountains, where they established new fiefdoms. So by AD 1372, when King Jayasthitimalla established the third Malla dynasty, Nepal had already been split into the three valley principalities of Patan, Bhatgaon and Kathmandu, and a clutch of feudal territories. By this time, the resident Newar population (whose origins are unknown), had emerged as artisans of considerable skill. Under the patronage of King Jayasthitimalla, and his successor, Yakshamalla, they forged a cultural renaissance and produced much of the exquisite stone and wood carving that adorn the Kathmandu valley today.

The empire that Yakshamalla divided amongst his sons in AD 1482, extended as far south as the Ganges river, encompassing Sikkim at the eastern end of the Himalayas. His sons managed to achieve a balance of power among themselves, but it was a delicate balance at best. During the next 200 years, the Malla hold over the valley gradually deteriorated and weakened .

Meanwhile, 50 miles to the west, the Gorkha Kingdom was growing under King Prithvi Narayan Shah, and in AD 1769 the Gorkhas conquered Kathmandu and moved their capital to the centre of the valley. From here, they sought to continue their expansionist drive,

such that by AD 1810, the Gorkha Kingdom stretched virtually across the Himalayas from Sikkim to Kashmir. However in AD 1790, their assault on Tibet was repulsed by Chinese forces, who also invaded Nepal two years later, forced a treaty on the Gorkhas and extracted the promise of a recurring tribute to their Emperor. In AD 1809, the Gorkhas lost a war against the Sikhs, and in AD 1816, the Gorkhas suffered defeat at the hands of the British and finally gave up their territorialist ambitions, and accepted the presence of a British resident.

While the 1816 treaty thwarted Gorkha expansion, it protected their commercial interests, and trade with both India and Tibet grew without interference. Nevertheless, Britain's subjugation of India must have been perceived as a threat to Nepal's independence. Jung Bahadur Rana, the general who usurped power from his Gorkha masters in AD 1846, was however able to dilute this threat by affecting a compromise with the British in AD 1860. Kathmandu accepted British 'guidance' on foreign policy, and allowed the British Indian army to recruit the Gorkha soldiers, who had demonstrated their valour during the border war. In return, Britain promised non-interference in internal affairs and guaranteed the Rana regime protection against external and internal enemies, including the Shah Kings, who were confined to their palace. To ensure the succession of his own line, the Rana declared his office hereditary and declared himself Maharajah. Protected and isolated from the changing world, the Rana regime strengthened their exploitative hold over Nepal, bestowing land and feudal rights on friends and relatives and neglecting the improvement of their agricultural economy. The Ranas, taking lessons in ostentation from European courts, built extravagant palaces and had Rolls Royces carried in over the mountain passes.

In 1947, when the Indian subcontinent was liberated from British rule, the Ranas lost their major prop. In the north, Chinese military muscle flexed to annex Tibet, calling into question Nepal's sovereign existence. Many Nepalis had served as political apprentices during India's freedom struggle. Rallying to a call for democracy in their own nation, they followed the Nepali Congress leader B.P. Koirala into guerilla warfare against the Ranas. Meanwhile, the nominal Shah monarch, King Tribhuvan, escaped to the Indian embassy in Kathmandu and later to India. When the Rana-republican war proved inconclusive, the two parties agreed to restore the Shah to his throne and presented him with a cabinet made up equally of Nepali Congress members and Rana nobles. The Rana Prime Minister, however, was forced into exile.

The parliamentary democracy that was the object of this exercise did not come forth immediately. During his four-year reign, King Tribhuvan was entirely successful in keeping the Nepali Congress away from any exercise of power. Even when his son, King Mahendra, announced the decision to hold elections, he managed to postpone them for four years. The nation finally went to the polls in February-March 1959. Voted in with a convincing majority, the Nepali Congress formed Nepal's first popular government. Its Prime Minister, B.P. Koirala, advocated democratic reforms and closer ties with India. King Mahendra saw himself being relegated into obscurity from which his dynasty had emerged only eight years earlier. In December 1960, he pre-empted any such situation, by banning all political parties and arresting Koirala and his cabinet. The parliament was thus dissolved, and democracy proved to be extremely short lived.

Pressurized by the persisting movement for democracy, the king was forced to call for elections, and democracy was finally restored.

II

GEOGRAPHY SEEMS to have bound the two nations together as both are part of the Gangetic basin. Their common religious and cultural heritage reflects this fact. So did the 1950 treaties of friendship and trade, allowing among other things, complete and reciprocal freedom of movement, residence and work for citizens of both countries. Today, an estimated 10 million people of Nepalese origin have struck roots in India. Correspondingly, in Nepal, Indian traders and businessmen have flourished.

Traditional techniques still dominate the agricultural sector which accounts for fifty-seven percent of the nation's output. It is no illusion that the picturesque rice fields of the Nepal countryside belong to an age gone by. They have seen no improvement in yields since the last twenty years, and marginal increases in food output have been swallowed by a rapid growth in population.

Industry too, is a victim of Nepal's history and constitutes only fourteen percent of her national product. Nepal's first motorable road was built as recently as 1956. To this date, much of her population lives in villages, many trekking days away from the nearest bus station. Even today, production of commercial energy is marginal, imposing its own constraints on the manufacturing sector.

In Nepal most of the industry is located in the Terai, the narrow fertile land running along the Indian border and in the Inner Terai, that lies at a slightly higher elevation. Separated by the Shivalik hills (2,500 to 5,000 feet), these two lowlands were once moist deciduous forests, largely made up of *sal (sharea robusta)*, that provided cover to elephants and tigers and to the great Indian rhino, who were driven out by wood cutters and poachers. Today they can only be seen in protected areas, such as the Royal Chitwan Park at the southern end of the Rapti valley.

North of the Inner Terai is the barren Mahabharat Lekh range (5,000 to 9,000 feet) that guards the Nepalese heartland, the mid-mountain valleys. These fertile inter-montane basins were once lakes, putting the geological stamp of credibility on legends of Kathmandu's origins. During the warm years of the Pleistocene epoch (from 2,50,000 to 10,000 years ago), melted glaciers filled the valley floors and deposited the alluvial soil that has nurtured rice fields for over a millenia.

Forming an emerald belt that runs west-northwest to east-southeast, these valleys yield immediately to the Nepal Himalayas, where Mount Everest is kept company by seven of the other world's highest peaks. Neither this formidable barrier, nor Mahabharat Lekh, however proved a deterrent to the stream of foreigners who, through the centuries, made

Kathmandu valley one of the richest ethno-cultural crucibles in the world. The original valley race is lost to history, which has only recorded its probable fusion into the Newar race. The Newaris are largely of Indo-Aryan stock, planted by early Kirati, Licchavi and Thakuri invaders, each of whom brought courtiers and soldiers who stayed and inter-married. From the east came Tibeto-Burmese migrants, and in the wake of King Tsrongtsong Gompo's invasion, Tibetan traders and settlers.

who took pride in tracing their ancestry to the Indian warrior caste of *Kshatriyas*. Their officers came of the same lineage and were the forebearers of today's *Chettris*. The people over whom they ruled and from whom they drew their Gorkha soldiers were however, largely Tibeto-Nepalese and included *Magars, Rais, Limbus,* and the *Gurungs* who inhabit the southern slopes of the Annapurna massif.

These Gorkha armies annexed the Indian regions of Garhwal and Kumaon, and later

A deep adherence to religious customs dominates the lives of the Nepalese.

When Newari artisans built the temples of the Malla era, their statues and symbols reflected the diversity of these cultural influences, thus integrating Hinduism, Buddhism and an earlier animism. Their language, Newari is also related both to the Indo-European family, spoken in the south, and to those of the Tibeto-Burmese, spoken in the north.

The national language, Nepali on the other hand, is a derivate of Sanskrit and was imposed on the country by the Shah dynasty,

fought the war against the British across the border. When they were finally defeated by General Ochterloney's troops, a tribute was paid to their fighting spirit by the General himself who allowed them to surrender with arms and colours. His recommendations prompted the British Indian army to put a clause in their 1816 Treaty with Nepal, granting the permission to recruit Gorkha fighting forces for itself. When Nepal was closed to foreigners, a Gorkha recruitment station was established at

Darjeeling, an Indian hill-station close to the Nepal border. Brandishing their gleaming *khukris* (curved knives), the Gorkhas helped the British Army quell the Indian Mutiny of 1857 and built their own reputation of fierce loyalty. Subsequently, they were formed into separate regiments, *corps d'elite* to which the best British officers were assigned. Fighting for the British in the First and Second World Wars, the Gorkhas earned thirteen Victoria Crosses. After 1947, eight Gorkha regiments were

Buddhism. Some of them, like the *Tamangs,* still appeal to their *shamans* to drive away the malevolent spirits of sickness and ill-fortune. But they have built *gompas* for their lamas and observe the Buddhist festivals. In their villages, prayer wheels turn the Buddhist texts and incense burns before *tangkhas.*

The best known of these mountain people are the Sherpas, highly reputed as mountain guides and climbers ever since Tenzing Norgay Sherpa accompanied Edmund Hillary on the

Nepali women are fond of wearing jewellery. Married women wear tihari, *a horizontal gold ornament strewn in red or green beads known as* pote.

Women in Nepal are usually seen dressed in the traditional guniu *or* fariya *and a* chowbandi choli.

incorporated into the Indian army. The British too, continue to treasure their fighting tradition and maintain four Gorkha regiments, which have fought many British battles in Cyprus and Gibraltar, Brunei and Malaysia and as far afield as the desolate Falklands.

The higher mountain reaches in the north of the country are more or less entirely populated by people of Tibetan descent, who practise

first successful expedition to Mount Everest. Their name, Tibetan or 'Easterner', reflects their origin in the Kham region of eastern Tibet. Buddhist, herders of yak and other mountain cattle, the Sherpas, would head for Nepal in

Following pages 24-25: *Stocky and hardworking, the Sherpas have learned to work and live alongside the arduous mountain ranges.*

23

the winters, bringing with them Tibetan salt and wool. When they returned to Tibet in spring, their yak herds would be packed with cloth, other manufactured goods and kerosene. To this day, some Sherpa tribes are semi-nomadic. In any case permanent settlement did not take place till the Sherpas learned to grow potato and barley, their staple food today.

Thus coupling agriculture, animal husbandry and trade, the Sherpas were among the more prosperous northern communities. When China closed the Tibet border after the Lhasa uprising of 1959, the Sherpas lost their trading income. The rapid growth in the climbing and trekking business that followed the opening of Nepal's borders was more than welcome. Victims of the realpolitik of one regime, the Sherpas became beneficiaries of the decision of another.

III

ON A CLEAR DAY, the Himalayas beckon from the Kathmandu's towers. For climbers from around the world, their challenging peaks are reason enough to journey to Nepal. For the less ambitious, their folds shelter glaciers and valleys, windswept monasteries and peaceful temples that make every trek a delightful voyage of discovery.

Half an hour south by air, or three days downstream on a bobbing raft, the elephant grass of the park still shields the majestic tiger and the great Indian rhino. But for most, Nepal is the Kathmandu valley, a treasure house of sculpture and architecture. Of the 114 monuments designated under the UNESCO'S World Heritage List, seven are in this tiny valley. Thousands of lesser temples, *stupas,* statues and buildings constitute a gallery that is aesthetically dazzling and culturally fascinating. Many of these exhibits remain uncatalogued or lie in crowded lanes or hamlets.

Facing page: An image of Seto Bhairavi, Durbar Square, Kathmandu.
Following pages 28-29: Powerfully classic in its geometry, the Bodhnath stupa has three terraces that ascend to its base, distinguishing it from all the other stupas in the valley.

Most are still part of everyday life—a visage of the elephant-headed, Lord Ganesh, daubed by the vermillion obeisance of daily devotees, or the gilded god of tooth-aches, Vaisha Dev, whose precincts are stuccoed with countless nails and petitions, hammered in by suffering believers, or the religious complex at the Swayambunath *stupa,* where at four every evening, trumpets and chanting signal the service of Buddhist monks. The monks, guardians of a site held sacred long before the time of the Buddha, reside in a *gompa* facing the monastery. A host of legends offer varying accounts of the early religiosity of the Swayambhu hillock. Most regard it as home to the gilded lotus, a manifestation of the Buddha godhead, while others speak of animist cults that were gathered here. The earliest recorded fact is of a monastery constructed here around AD 41 by Manadeva I.

Between then and the mid-thirteenth century, little is known about the *stupa.* In AD 1234, a Tibetan monk, Dharmasu journeyed to the valley, and spend eight years here. His biography contains details of the *stupa* and establishes that Swayambunath had emerged as a major centre of Buddhist teaching. Later accounts are chiefly of the *stupa's* destruction by the ravages of nature, and in AD 1346, by Shams-ud-din Ilyas' troops. On this occasion, it took twenty-six years to restore Swayambunath. The bronze and gilt work was entrusted to artisans in Kathmandu. When completed, all of Kathmandu celebrated: the town was illuminated for four days and a large procession carried the engraved metal work to the *stupa* for installation.

Time and again, Hindu royalty paid for the construction of this Buddhist shrine. Epitomizing a happy blend of Hinduism and *Tantrism* with the teachings of the Buddha, are the exquisite Ganga and Yamuna bronzes that guard the eternal flame, the *vajra* (thunderbolt) that stands at the head of the steps, flanked by the Hindu temples. Built by King Pratapamalla in the mid-seventeenth century, the temples are an exception to the strictly north-south orientation of the *stupa.* This is no geometrical mistake, the King sited them for their symmetry about the north-west axis, looking from

Kathmandu, from where he also built a road, a bridge across the Bishnumati and the enormous stairway to the top of the hill.

For the rest, the *stupa is* a study in Buddhist formalism—the five mystic Buddhas, one each in niches at the four cardinal points and one facing the stairs. The huge hemispherical mound represents the basic elements of nature: earth, fire, air and water, while the thirteen gilded rings of the spire represent the various levels of consciousness, ascending to *nirvana*

History and legend too, set Bodhnath apart from other Buddhist structures in the valley. Built along the old trade route to Tibet, its renovation was almost always funded by the Lhasa regime, perhaps in homage to an important Tibetan *lama* over whose grave the *stupa* is said to have been built. History adduces no evidence of the Bodhnath *stupa* being linked to Newari Buddhist festivals. To this date it is worshipped only by Buddhists of the Tibetan persuasion—Sikkimese, Ladakhis,

The eyes painted on the stupa of Swambunath monastery are always open, epitomizing the vigilance of the deity over the people of Nepal.

which is represented by the umbrella at the peak.

Even more formal and powerfully classic in its geometry, is the larger Bodhnath *stupa,* three miles to the east. The three terraces that ascend to its base distinguish Bodhnath from all the other *stupas* in the valley. So does the absence of the meditating *(dhyani)* Buddhas. Instead, small images of the *Amitabh* Buddha (108 of them), are set into the base of the *stupa.*

Bhutanese, Sherpas and the refugees who have carved a tiny piece of Tibet around the *stupa,*

Facing page: *The Swambunath temple—the most common regard is that it is home to the gilded lotus, a manifestation of the Buddha godhead. Yet the exquisite Ganga and Yamuna bronzes that guard the eternal flame and the* vajra *(thunderbolt) bespeak of the happy coexistence of Hinduism and Tantrism with the teachings of the Buddha.*

selling brass and silver trinkets, weaving their carpets, and brewing their rice beer.

Another later wave of foreigners have left their mark on Kathmandu. In the late sixties, 'Love, Peace, Gurus' and *hashish* were in, and the hippy trail led all the way from the expensive suburbs of the industrial West to the crowded alleys of Kathmandu. Then came the hard-nosed materialism of the seventies and then the warfare in the Persian Gulf and the Afghanistan mountains. The hippy trail dried up, and so did the acid rock and the many *mantras* of love and peace. What remained was an assortment of pie-shops, bakeries and cheap lodges, Tibetan cafes and eateries like 'The Lunch Box' and 'Aunt Jane's Kitchen'. Today, many have shifted north, from Freak Street and New Road to Thamel, where they rub shoulders with the more ritzy establishments that serve everything from tortillas to sukiyaki, and borscht (introduced to the valley by Boris Lissanevitch, patron saint of Nepalese hoteliers). In the early 1950s, his 'Royal Hotel' was the country's only western hostelry. When the 'Royal Hotel' closed, its 'Yak and Yeti' restaurant moved to Darbar Marg. The 'Chimney Restaurant', located on the landscaped lawns of the 'Yak and Yeti' hotel, still boasts of the famous copper fireplace of its parent, and its fine Russian cuisine. Its neighbour, the 'Naachghar', offers succulent game cooked in traditional Rana style and served in the rococo splendour of what was once their private theatre.

The European influence on Nepalese architecture was part of the baggage that Jung Bahadur Rana carried back from a trip to England and France in AD 1850. From then on, pseudo-baroque was *de rigeur* among the Rana nobility. On scale alone, the Rana's Palace, Singha Durbar must rank as being the masterpiece of this period. Littered with crystal chandeliers, marble baths and all other confections of the style, this 1700 roomed structure was built by Shamsher Rana in 1901. Capacious enough for both his personal and official needs, after 1951 it housed the offices of King Tribhuvan's Central Government. However, only the main wing survived the fire of 1933. Since restored, the Singha Durbar today houses the Prime Minister's office and the National Planning Commission.

From here, it's a short stroll past the National Archives to Kalmochan temple on the left bank of the Bagmati river. Built in AD 1852, to commemorate the war against the British, Kalmochan is the only surviving edifice, exemplifying a synthesis of Hindu-Mughal architecture. Despite this, and the exquisite carved wood mythological friezes, few visitors visit the temple or the Pachali Bhairava temple, ten minutes downstream. Encircled by the roots of a *pipal* tree, the brass image in the temple depicts one of the manifestations of Lord Shiva, which is assumed to be keeping watch over his companion, Vishnu—the King of Nepal. The monarch makes an offering at the temple on designated days to express his gratitude.

But the temples more popularly associated with Nepalese royalty lie two kilometres to the north, in the celebrated Durbar Square area. The Taleju temple, in particular, owes its gilded magnificence to the medieval belief that the king derived his earthly powers from the goddess Taleju Bhawani. Originally she resided in Bhaktapur, whose monarch supposedly possessed a *mantra* (sacred chant) through which his power flowed. The *mantra* was, obviously, a precious heirloom, normally passed from the king to his eldest son just before his assumption. However, Ratnamalla, the ambitious youngest son of Yakshamalla, tricked his father into revealing the magic syllables to him. The story goes that, despite his duplicity, the *mantras* worked and Ratnamalla was able to invoke a visitation by the goddess. She sent him to Kathmandu, then under Thakuri Kings, and bid him enlist the support of their Minister. Contact was established the very next day. At a poisoned last supper, the Minister supervised the premature end of his employers and Ratnamalla assumed power. The goddess was rewarded with the construction of the Tarani Devi temple and the renegade Minister with death.

Facing page: Akash Bhairav. *This gold mask normally covered, is exposed during the seven-day* Indrajatra *festival, literally the procession of Lord Indra.*

Intricately carved windows and statues still decorate the temple, the first to be built in the Durbar Square area. Ratnamalla probably built himself a palace in the neighbourhood, which soon replaced Kasthamandap, the house of wood, as the focus of the town. Today, one is most likely to approach Durbar Square via the wide thoroughfare of New Road, the commercial artery of Kathmandu. Before the 1933 earthquake which cleared the way for its construction, most trading was carried out

crowded, but is nonetheless impressive, to say the least.

The existing Taleju temple was built in AD 1562, the first to violate the ceiling height, traditionally set by the two-storeyed Pashupatinath temple. Its builder, Mahendramalla set it upon a huge stepped platform and gave it a three-tiered roof, motivated by the desire that the temple be visible from the old home of the goddess in Bhaktapur. Even higher are the towers of the

A statue of Hanuman, at the Durbar Square in Kathmandu.

along the old India-Tibet track. It still exists, a crowded road that points east-northeast, running from the Bishnumati bridge, past Kasthamandap and Durbar Square to Asan Tole. For centuries, most of Kathmandu's religious buildings came up on or around this road. As a result, the area became a stockyard of temples, one that could have been far more pleasing if it had been less

Facing page: Samyak *festival, Kathmandu.*

Durbar Square, that look onto the Himalayan snows and down into the courtyards of the Royal Palace. In the largest of these courtyards, a king once danced in dedication to Nasal, the dancing form of Lord Shiva. Pratapamalla (AD 1641-1674), named the fifty-five metre long courtyard Nasal Chowk, after the divine King of Dance, and invited other performers onto its central stage. The later kings were coronated here and lived in the rooms that look upon it. Today, the King lives in the Royal Palace,

located to the north of the city. The Nasal Chowk comes alive only once a year, on the ninth day of *Dasain,* the ten-day long festival in September or October.

Just outside its blue, green and gold gates, swathed in a cloak of fine red cloth, a statue of the monkey god Hanuman stands to one side. Its stone pedestal is always strewn with offerings of grain and coins. Elsewhere in the area, believers pay obeisance to a fierce Kal (black) Bhairava, dropping their offerings into a skull bowl, and at the Ashok Binayak shrine, the elephant-god Ganesh wishes travellers godspeed. At the steps of their temple, under the seventeenth century erotica and twentieth century signboards, vendors peddle fresh vegetables, dried fish, fragrant flowers and incense sticks, while children happily pose for photographs asking for 'One rupee please'.

One child who may not be photographed however is the Kumari, the living goddess, whose home is just off the square, in the Kumari Bahal, set around an eighteenth century courtyard. Some of the finest wood-work decorates the walls of the courtyard and frames the shutters of the upper windows, from which she makes her fleeting appearances. Since Jaiprakashmalla installed the first Kumari in this house, the institution of the 'virgin goddess' has been an unbroken one.

Driven from his throne, King Jaiprakashmalla found refuge in the temple of Guhyeshvari. With the help of the resident deity, the first Kumari helped restore him to his throne. Since then, the Kumari has been regarded as the human form of the royal goddess, Taleju Bhawani, inextricably linking the fate of Nepal's monarch with her. When she is selected at the age of four or five, her horoscope must agree with that of the King. Once she is installed, she remains the Kumari until she reaches puberty. Every year, she renews her blessing to the King. The ritual at her house precedes a mammoth procession, through streets lined with people surging forward to pay their respects to her. Atop her filigreed gold and silver chariot,

Facing page: The Kumari *or the Living Goddess rides into the streets of Kathmandu, in a gilded chariot.*

the richly ornamented Kumari is a statue of serenity. She is drawn from the Buddhist Sakya clan of goldsmiths, thus show-casing the Nepalese harmony between Hinduism and Buddhism.

Paraded in flesh and blood, or enshrined in metal or stone, Kathmandu's gods and goddesses are by no means confined to the Durbar Square area. Further up the old Tibet route, or just off it, lie many stops for the temple gazer—the first floor shrine dedicated to Akash Bhairava, the road-side niche for a brass Ganesh, the *tantric* Lunchun Lunbun Ajima temple, where pictures of the King and Queen are flanked by erotica, and the Seto Macchendranath shrine.

Complemented by splendid tympana, door frames, copper prayer wheels and bells, the gilded copper roof of the Macchendranath temple is a huge golden ornament, severely mutilated by robbers, and now protected by a cage. Lions and griffins guard access to the resident statue of Avalokitesvara, a Buddhist deity also worshipped by Hindus.

The Seto Macchendranath is one of the few Buddhist monuments within the town. Another smaller Macchendranath temple near Lagan Khel, has gained importance through the annual visit of the Seto Macchendranath deity during a festival in late March. Also basking in reflected glory is the *stupa* of Srigha Chaitya, a smaller replica of Swayambunath, considered equally important by pilgrims physically unfit to climb up to the higher sanctum of Swayambunath.

The Pashupatinath temple, considered to be one of the most important Shiva shrines in the subcontinent, attracts devotees from the remotest corners of Nepal and India. Situated five kilometres away from Kathmandu, Pashupatinath is on the banks of the Bagmati river, which is considered holy, as it merges with the river Ganga downstream. Cleansed by the obligatory dip in the river, devotees pay obeisance to the stone *lingam* (phallus) in the sanctum, erected in AD 1359. The earliest recorded structure on the spot was a three-storeyed temple, built in AD 1412 by Jayajyotimalla. After it was damaged, Bhupendramalla built the two-tiered pagoda that stands even today, aided by countless

Top (left & right): *Two-dimensional stone statues of epic Hindu gods accompanied by mythical animals and attendants, belonging to the baroque epoch in Nepalese art, that is the renaissance that took place between the fourteenth and eighteenth century.* ***Bottom (left):*** *Details from a Bhaktapur Torana,   a semi-circular tympanum leaning forward and crowned by a Garuda;* ***(right):*** *Intricately carved wooden Torana at Patan's Durbar Square.*

Top (left & right): *The focus of Nepalese sculptural art has been the human form—male and female in the form of gods and goddesses, both bedecked with jewellery. The female form being slender with protuding, rounded breasts and a heart shaped face, while the male form is more fleshy.* ***Bottom (left & right):*** *Erotic carvings on a temple strut. Most temple struts in Nepal have erotic carvings, patterned after the stone pillars of ancient Hindu temples.*

modifications and restorations that make it impossible to ascertain the age of any individual part of the structure.

Following the ancient tradition existing in Varanasi, the bathing ghats of Pashupatinath are only on the west bank, designed possibly to enable rituals to be dedicated to the rising sun. A weir ensures that the holy water is always available to bathers and to the mourners who sprinkle it onto cremation pyres.

At the Dakshinkali temple, the ancient ritual of animal sacrificial offerings to the goddess Kali still takes place twice a week. The temple, which is believed to guard the valley against incursions from the south, was built by Pratapamalla in the fourteenth century. But the sacrificial site which constitutes the forested depths of a narrow mountain gorge seems to have been designed by nature itself.

IV

THE RICHNESS OF Kathmandu's religion and culture makes it easy to forget that it is also located in an exquisitely picturesque valley spotted with meadows, forests, gorges and ridges forming a ring-side seat on the Himalayas.

Of these ridges, Nagarkot, has become a popular resort, with hotels catering to tourists who are eager to watch the sunrise over the Himalayas—a spectacular show of shade and light that begins with Makalu and Everest in the distant east and travels, rose and gold, to Annapurna and Dhaulagiri, the craggy giants in the west. Just beyond the valley there is Dhulikhel, which offers sunrise views from the terraced lawns of a posh hotel, or from temples that seem to have been sited just for the purpose. To the south, named after the flowers *(phul)* that cover its slopes in spring, is the Phul Chowki summit, that looks down on the entire valley, and beyond to the Himalayas.

Facing page: The statue is that of the guardian deity of Nyatapola temple, built by Raja Bhupatindra Malla in 1708 AD at Bhaktapur.
Following pages 42-43: The beautiful snow-capped Himalayas where the gods and goddesses are said to reside look down upon the Kathmandu valley.

To the north, beyond the Royal Game Reserve is the Nagarjuna hill, crowned by a Buddhist *chaitya.*

Most of these nature outings can be combined with visits to temples and shrines. From Nagarkot, for example, it is a gentle walk along the eastern ridge to Changu Narayana, where the valley's earliest of settlements are thought to have been located. A temple of Vishnu, which is believed to have been in existence since the fourth century, is sited here. The ornate, main temple is less than three hundred years old, but in and around it are innumerable statues dating back to earlier centuries. The most celebrated is a Lichhavi masterpiece belonging to the fifth century—a life size statue of Vishnu's mount, Garuda, in human form. From the same period is a partially damaged, yet exquisite statue of Vishnu, with his ten arms and heads. Particularly interesting however is the tenth century statue of Vishnu, that became the prototype for countless statues and paintings in later centuries. Flanked by his wife Lakshmi, and his mount Garuda, it clearly depicts his four attributes—a lotus, a mace, a discus and a conch. This conch is said to have been the inspiration for the layout of Bhaktapur, the ninth century city founded by King Anandamalla. Its streets do unwind, taking the shape of a double S, however, their orientation is unlikely to be by design, since Anandamalla did not build the city from the ground up, but integrated the existing settlements into a city.

Whatever the truth, all the legends surrounding Bhaktapur are essentially Hindu. The city is said to be protected by female goddesses—Taleju, the Ashtamatrikas (eight mother goddesses), and the nine incarnations of Durga. Taleju was shifted here in AD 1326 from her earlier residence in Simraongarh. The new shrine, Mul Chowk, became the epicentre for a wave of Hindu orthodoxy. King Jayasthitimalla, the leading light of the Malla Dynasty, decided to rule the valley from the adjacent palace and reorganised Bhaktapur along caste lines. Residential areas were demarcated for each caste, their houses built to a prescribed design, and even their tax dues were thus determined. In a final gesture of

preservation, his successor, Yakshamalla (AD 1428-1482) built a wall around the entire city. The plateau around the Taleju temple was favoured with fortress battlements, behind which the Durbar Square area developed.

Going by photographs and etchings from the early part of the century, this development was haphazard and cluttered. The 1933 earthquake razed many of these buildings to the ground, and today, Bhaktapur's Durbar Square is sparse and open. The entrance to the palace visible from the south end of the Square. Erected by Ranjitmalla to commemorate his conquest of Dudh Kosi and Dolkha, the Sundhoka (golden gate) is justifiably the most famous in the valley, with an archway occupied by a majestic representation of the resident deity: the sixteen-armed Taleju.

Facing the deity, with hands folded in prayer, is a life-size statue of Bhupatindramalla, also erected by his son, Ranjitmalla. The pillar that supports him is somewhat disproportionate and squat in comparison with those built before it in Kathmandu and Patan. In fact, the know-how for erecting such pillars was restricted to a few artisans in Kathmandu, and Ranjitmalla had to appeal to King Jaiprakashmalla for permission to import the technology. While acquiescing, the Kathmandu monarch bid the experts ensure that the exercise was not successful. It so happened that the column fell while being erected. The salvage job undertaken by the artisans forced a diminution in aesthetics, but it did keep both the royal patrons happy!

Before Ranjitmalla built the Sundhoka gate, the entrance to the palace was probably on the western side of the facade. However, little remains to trace the Newari influence after consequent renovations undertaken by the Ranas. Thankfully a delightful selection of Newari paintings is seen in the museum collection. The eastern facade, famous for its fifty five windows of the finest fret work, escaped modernisation. Though the 1933 earthquake destroyed most of the wood work, many windows have been excellently restored.

The Sundhoka gate marks the cleft between the west and east facades and affords access to the Sadasiva Chowk, which serves as a forecourt to the Taleju Chowk. Richly carved and decorated in consonance with its strategic importance to Nepalese royalty, the Taleju Chowk is banned to non-Hindus. Much of its ornamentation was done during Jitamitramalla's (AD 1673-1696) reign, who had the entrance adorned with statues of himself and his wife. He also knocked a hole in the eastern wall of the chowk, and built an impressive portal that suggests a temple entrance, but leads instead to another small courtyard, that is the Kumari Chowk dedicated to the Ashtamatrikas. The physical contiguity of the two chowks echoes the spiritual synergy between Taleju and the other goddesses of the valley.

The most reclusive of these resides in the Nyatapola temple. The name of the temple, which simply means five storeys, offers no clue to the identity of the deity. All we know is that she is a *tantric* goddess, installed in the dead of the night by King Bhupatindramalla himself. An oft repeated lore suggests that, he had built a shrine dedicated to Bhairava, that still stands in the same square. The deity faced west, to protect his city from marauders. Unfortunately, Bhairava proved malefic and caused great disturbances. *Tantric* priests were called in. As a countervailing force, they advised the installation of the mysterious goddess, to whom even her priestly caretakers may tend only in the dark.

Hundreds of little bells tinkle from Nyatapola's five roofs, supported by 108 richly carved wooden struts. The temple is a felicitous exercise in symmetry—its square platform exactly thrice as wide as the sanctum, the five roofs matched by five receding plinths below. At each level of the plinth, a pair of massive stone figure guards the central stairway, each pair ten times as powerful as the one immediately below. The goddesses above the griffins, the lions, the elephants and the wrestlers, Jayamalla and Bhata, in turn ten times as strong as the average man.

These strong men were to become a popular pair. In AD 1860, their likenesses were set up

Facing page: Details of the Tusha hitti (water fountain) of Patan, earlier used as the royal bath. Interesting to note here is the conch shaped tap.

in front of the Dattatreya temple, that dominates Bhaktapur's oldest square, Techupal Tole, north-east of the Durbar Square area. The Dattatreya temple probably doubled as a meeting place for the community and for Tibetan traders. Its resident deity was, and is, worshipped by both Hindus and Buddhists, and is one of the few Bhaktapur shrines admitting Buddhist influence. The other at Jaur Bahl, on the road south to the Hanumante river, is home to a meditating Buddha. But Techupal

government in the distant northwest, that is the Federal Republic of Germany. Work on the Dattatreya temple and Square constituted the first phase of the Bhaktapur Development Project, which extended to water supply and drainage, and to the creation of job opportunities through wood crafts and carpet weaving.

Near Patan, Swiss assistance has helped set up a handicrafts centre for Tibetan refugees. At Jawlakhel near the Patan zoo, busy fingers

The tradition of wearing masks to celebrate the Gaijatra *festival, it is believed began as a result of a king's efforts to entertain his queen, who was distraught at the death of their son.*

Tole itself is surrounded by evidences of Hindu religious activity, and a host of its buildings have been used as *maths* or residences for Hindu priests. One of them, Pujari Math, boasts of the famous 'peacock' window, a fine example of seventeenth century woodcarving. At one time the Tibetan Government used to send yearly gifts to this *math*.

Today, the square on which it stands has been renovated by the munificence of another

conjure up the traditional dragon motif on rugs and carpets that may be shipped directly to a European wholesaler, or sold at one of the colourful shops in the neighbourhood. On every wall, the friendly face of the Dalai Lama signifies the solidarity of the Tibetan community.

It is appropriate that Patan should host the Tibetan refugee camp, for it is redolent with Buddhist tradition and monuments. The oldest of these are reputed to be the four, so called Ashoka *stupas* . Reputed because they have never been subjected to scientific dating—who would want to run the risk of shattering such a magnificent legend? In Ashoka's supposed scheme of things, the *stupas* demarcated the city and set at the four coordinates, guarded it against evil from all directions. The two axes suggested then also sketched Patan's main roads. Their intersection provided the site for the Durbar Square area.

its monasteries and Buddhist shrines. It was a shock from which Patan was never to recover: from the capital city of a kingdom, it deteriorated into a suburb of Kathmandu, where the Rana's nobles sited their baroque villas.

Though much of Patan's Buddhist architecture has been lost forever, the buildings that came up in their stead exemplify the finest of Newari architecture. Built on the site of the Hatko Vihara is Mul Chowk, former home of

The Gaijatra *festival is celebrated with humour and political and social satire. Puppet shows and plays are staged to mock the monarchy and the bureaucracy.*

Unfortunately, it will never be known what magnificent Buddhist shrines stood here or what the fifth central *stupa,* which was probably located in the vicinity, looked like. The ravages of time and Malla reconstructions have taken their toll. What was left was destroyed by Prithvi Narayan Shah's plundering armies in AD 1762. While the Gorkha King conquered the entire valley, his troops came down particularly hard on Patan and ravaged

the Patan royal family, guarded in the north by the shrine of Taleju. The first Degutal temple was built here by Hariharasinhamalla, who ruled the city for his father, King Shivasinhamalla (AD 1578-1620). But the exquisite brass images of Ganga and Yamuna and the gilded *torana* or tympanum, with the Asthamatrikas (the eight mother goddesses), that today adorn the temple were sponsored by Srinivasamalla. He rebuilt most of the Durbar

Square area after it was destroyed by a fire in AD 1663. To this phase of reconstruction also belongs the deeply etched and fabulously detailed sunken bath, the Tusha Hiti, in the southern most courtyard, the Sundari Chowk. Patan's most contentious piece of construction, however, was erected by its next king, Yoganarendramalla. Inspired by the Pratapamalla pillar in Kathmandu, the King perched likenesses of himself and his son atop a pillar facing the Degutal temple, invoking the blessings of goddess Taleju. Thereby, he aroused the jealousy of the Bhaktapur King, Bhupatindramalla, now left to preside over the only valley city without its own pillar. Unable to commission a stone mason to rectify matters, he recruited a Brahmin to curse his rival's son. The son died, and depending on which legend one chooses to believe, the saddened father either became a wandering hermit, or was poisoned on a trip to Changu Narayana.

The third courtyard, the Mani Keshav Narayan Chowk, stands on the site of a Lichhavi Palace, the Mani Gala, dating back to AD 643. Its richly carved facade yields to a museum of eighteenth century bronzes and woodwork. It also hosts an interesting window, surrounded by a highly ornamented gilded frame. Below it is the front piece of a throne, with a Garuda in the centre. Above it arch the hoods of intertwined cobras. The centrepiece is a standing Avalokitesvara, the compassionate Buddha. When the King decided to appear before the populace, the centrepiece would be removed and he would mount the throne, appearing as a Buddha godhead or as an incarnation of Vishnu.

Statues of other *avtaars* of Vishnu constitute the Char Narayana temple, on the opposite side of the square. Next to it is the unusual, black stone, Krishna Mandir. Its ground floor is a pillared hall; its first floor bordered by eight stone pavilions, houses the deity; on the second floor, these are echoed by a tighter cluster of identical pavilions, from which the main *shikhara* emerges—an authentic Indian

Facing page: Gopal Krishna temple in Patan. Painted on its walls are some exquisite sixteenth century epic friezes.

spire in a profoundly Newari square.

The heavily ornamented Kwa Bahal monastery of Patan, lies just off the Durbar Square. Set in a 40 ft x 40 ft courtyard, the tiny shrine is raised upon a stone platform. Twelve carved wooden pillars support the wooden roof, entirely cloaked by copper and gilt, and rising to a tiny thirteen-ringed spire. Small though it is, the ornate shrine holds many excellent statues including those of Buddha godheads, meditating *(dhyani)* Buddhas, and of supplicants kneeling before the image of Gautam Buddha.

Buddhist influences can, infact, be found on any of the four roads leading off the Square. The southern axis leads to the Lagan *stupa,* the largest of the four Ashoka *stupas.* Flat and overgrown with grass, it lacks the *Harmika,* that is the cube customarily placed atop the *stupa.* Instead, a small mortar *stupa,* dedicated in AD 1878, houses four Buddhas in tiny niches. Just off the road to this primitive structure is the Rato (red) Macchendranath, counterpart to Kathmandu's Seto, (white) Macchendranath, and worshipped by both Hindus and Buddhists.

To the east and west lie identical flat earthen mounds, also considerably embellished by restorations in the last two centuries. The road north, leads to the only Ashoka *stupa* with a mortared surface. It has the *Harmika* with eyes on all the four sides, a thirteen tiered spire and four Buddhas, all of which were probably installed much after Ashoka's rule. Just south of this *stupa is* Patan's oldest temple, the five roofed Kumbhesvar temple, dedicated in AD 1392 to the bronze *chaturmukha* (four faced) *linga.* There are four doors to the sanctum, each guarded by two of the Ashtamatrikas. For the main western door, this honour goes to Indrayani and Varahi.

Two hundred kilometers to the west, on Pokhara's Phewa lake, a leafy island shelters a temple dedicated to the same mother goddess, Varahi. But only the locals visit it. The foreigners who come to Pokhara are on a different kind of pilgrimage—to the majesty of the Himalayas. Annapurna, one of the world's highest peaks, is only fifty kilometers away. Even closer is Macchapuchhare, the Fish Tail

peak. Though only 6967 meters high and a mere thirty kilometres from Pokhara, it dominates the horizon.

V

WITH THIS KIND OF setting, it seemed natural that Pokhara should become the trekking capital of Nepal—sixty per cent of international trekkers in Nepal walk into the Annapurana region, north of Pokhara. The tourist areas along the airport road and near the lake are dotted with trekking agencies which can arrange everything, from trekking permits to trained porters.

Yet, trekking independently in these parts is feasible—thanks to well marked trails. Inns run by the Thakatl people make it possible to travel without food and tents. Along Nepal's most popular trek, to Jomosom and Muktinath, the inns have long serviced wayfarers to the North.

The Kathmandu-Pokhara road was opened only in the early seventies, yet Pokhara is already littered with the plastic signs of the twentieth century. Within hours, the trekker to Jomosom climbs past these, following the Yamdi river west into the rice fields and the stone walls of unspoiled villages. In the liquid light of the mountains, pastoral life is captured in its timeless form; plodding cattle threshing the newly sickled rice, worn hands pounding maize in stone mortars and the glowing embers of the sun-baked dung cakes at eventide. Past the thatched roofs of these hamlets, the trail leads up to Naudanda. Here, perched on a ridge, 1458 metres high, one can view the day's progress, at Pokhara, almost 600 meters below. Through pine and rhododendron, the climb leads to the pass at Khare, then down to tramp the rocky shale along the Modir river. After the long and arduous trudge, a series of waterfalls at Birethanti offer respite.

Onward and upward the trail winds through dense forests, past views of Annapurna South, and the perfect cone of Macchapucchare,

Facing page: On a clear day . . . The Macchapuchhare, meaning 'Fishtail', of the Annapurna group, clearly visible from Pokhara.

unclimbed in deference to the Gurung's reverence for it. From Ghodepani pass at 2,900 metres or further up from Pun Hill, one can get a dazzling view of the entire Annapurna massif. From here the trail winds down through Magar and the Hindu villages, to the sulphur springs of Tatopani (hot water) on the Kali Gandaki river. Past its rushing waters, the trail climbs north through a steep gorge that cuts right through the Himalayas. Between the towering peaks of Dhaulagiri and Annapurna, (both more than 8000 metres above sea level), the Kali Gandaki carves the earth's deepest canyon. Through it the trek climbs to the trans-Himalayan plateau that continues past the border region into Tibet. The indigent or rushed, can fly into this arid region, landing at Jomosom. From here it is a hard day's climb to Muktinath, where below a snowy ridge, Hindus and Buddhists worship the flame that burns at the mouth of a spring. From Muktinath, one can climb east to the Thorong La pass at 5416 metres and walk through yak pasture land into the Manang valley.

Further east, the trekker passes through the stone huts of Manang villages, leaving the Glacier Dome (7193 metres) and Tilicho Peak to the west. And then, as the Marsyangdi river turns south, the trail follows it through terraced fields to Dumre on the Kathmandu—Pokhara road. On heading back down the Kali Gandaki, a leisurely climb to the glittering Dhaulagiri ice-fall offers a view of the Annapurna, Tilicho and Tukche peaks across the gorge.

South of Dhaulagiri, another track heads west across the Kali Gandaki and along its tributary Magyandi. Through forests, it climbs across the Jaljali ridge, on to the summer pasture of Dhopatan. North of it lies Tarakot, once the capital of the medieval kingdom of Tichurong. Beyond it, the boundaries of the Shep Phuksundo National Park protect the Phuksundo lake and the elusive snow leopard. Closed to foreigners in early 1974, parts of the park have recently been opened to trekkers. Further north, perched at 4,500 metres atop Crystal mountain, are two ancient *stupas* that probably attracted pilgrims long before Buddhism came to Tibet—this is evident by the pre-Buddhist iconography, as well as by the thousands of ancient prayer stones that surround the monastery.

In Nepal's Eastern Himalayas, a whole generation of trekkers have trudged over passes and across rivers to reach another fabled monastery, the Thyangboche. In the month of November, on a full moon night, masked dances are performed in its courtyard to celebrate the *Mani Rimdu* festival. Unfortunately the monastery was destroyed by a fire in January 1989, but aided by Sir

takes just forty minutes, landing at an airfield above the main trail. From here Thyangboche is another day's climb up the Dudh Kosi river past Namche Bazaar, the Sherpa village. Most trekkers turn back from here, but for those with more time and stronger lungs, the best view of Everest is still three days away, at Kala Patthar, (black rock). The hill although 5545 metres high, is dwarfed by its gigantic neighbours, Everest, Lhotse, Changtse and the Nuptse.

Even more arduous is the trek into the

The Thyangboche monastery perched on a ridge and surrounded by the Everest, Lhoste and Ama Dablam, enjoys an exotic location at an altitude of 4000 metres.

Edmund Hillary and the Himalayan Trust, the Sherpa community has ensured its successful reconstruction.

The surface route to Thyangboche starts with a day-long bus ride from Kathmandu to Jiri, at 1900 metres, moving across three passes—the Thodung at 3090 metres, Lamjura at 3530 metres and Tragsindho at 3080 metres. An experienced trekker would take at least seven days to reach Lukla, whereas the air traveller

Hongu region, a river valley to the south-east of the Everest. Few trekkers make the effort to climb over the Mera La Pass (5415 metres) into this area which offers a majestic view of the Everest, Makalu and Kanchenjunga. On the other side of the Khumbu region, south-west of the Everest, is another remote area, the

Facing page: *Namche Bazaar, the prosperous capital of the Sherpas in Khumbu.*

The rapid passage of clouds adds an alluring grey shade to the early evening hue cast over the Langthang range.

The snow-clad massif, of Dhaulagiri, meaning 'white mountain' rising to a height of 8167 metres dominates the surrounding valleys of Nepal.

The Manaslu range meaning 'mountain of the spirit' stands 8163 metres tall.

The Nuptse, which stands at an altitude of 7879 metres in the Everest area of Nepal.

Annapurna III. Even on the highest of Himalayan peaks as this, it is possible to detect the unmistakable traces of a past at the bottom of the ocean.

The intimidating Lhotse, which stands 8501 metres above sea level, in close proximity to Mt. Everest.

Rolwaling (furrow), named thus for the narrow rock opening from which the river pours into its valley. Largely uninhabited, Rolwaling came to public notice when Eric Shipton photographed a yeti track on a glacier in the northern part of the valley. Other climbers too, have documented similar tracks, but the existence of the yeti is still to be proved.

The climb to Rolwaling is a daunting one, but the rewards come early with the unobstructed view of Gauri Shankar, the offers both a bird's eye view of the valley and of the mountains from Burlang Bhanjyang. From here one climbs past primitive *chortens* (prayer flags), and walls engraved with the hallowed words *Om Mani Padme Hum*, to Kutumsang. Then via Tharepati, descending through rhododendron and oak forests inhabited by langurs, reach the prosperous village of Melamchigaon. The fifth day's trek takes one to Tarkhegyang village. Rather than return the way one came, it would make sense

The light of the moon illuminates the sacred slopes of Ama Dablam, which at a height of 6856 metres looms over the entire Khumbu valley.

mountain held in reverence by both Buddhists and Hindus, to whom its twin peaks represent Lord Shiva and his wife, Parvati.

Those intimidated by the rarefied altitudes of these regions, would do well to consider walking into the Helambu area, north of Kathmandu, which offers a good exposure both to Himalayan trekking and to the Sherpa people. Starting from the picnic spot at Sundari Jal, north-east of Kathmandu, the first day's trail to head through the forests to Sermathang, in the heart of an apple growing area, just two days north of Panchkhal, on the China road.

One could also head back east to Tharepat,

Following pages 56-57: *The Everest, as if warmed up by the light of the setting sun.*
Pages 58-59: *Thumserku Peak by night. This picture perfectly illustrates that the grandeur of the Himalayas increases manifold at night.*

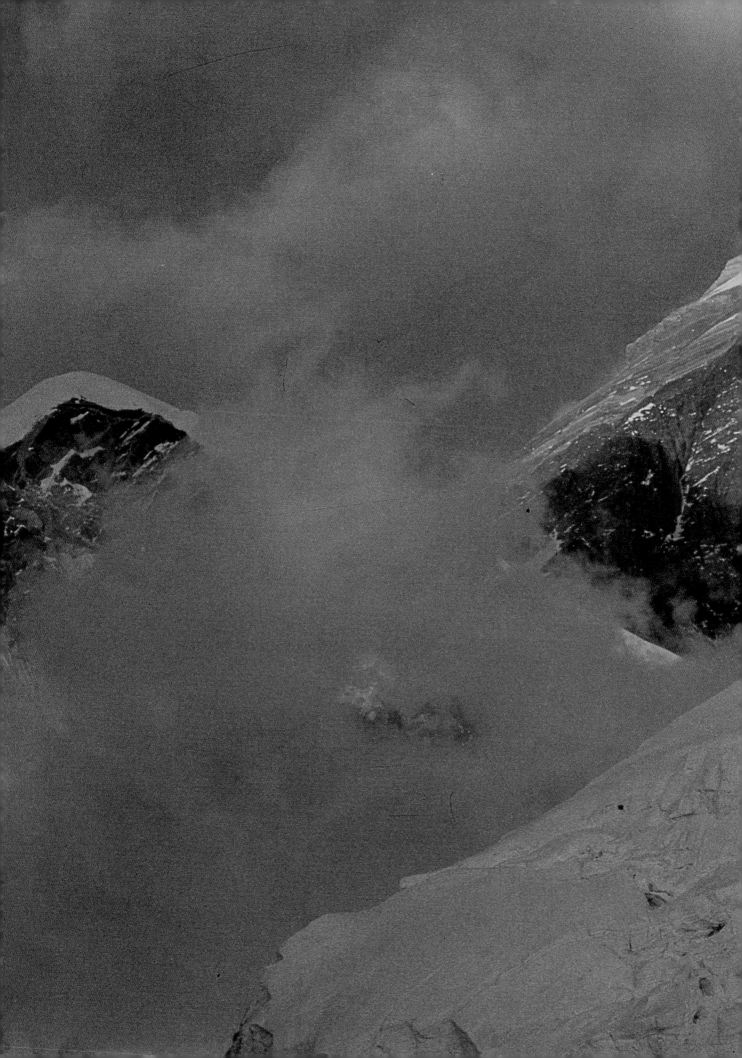

and in a hard day's walk, follow the ridge to the sacred Gosainkund lakes, at 4400 metres. For years pilgrims have followed another route to Gosainkund, which is said to have been formed when Lord Shiva plunged his *trishul* (trident) into the mountains. This congested path climbs from Trisuli Bazaar towards the Langtang region, turning east at Dhunche. One could of course do it the other way round, and head down from the holy lakes to Dhunche, a two day's walk past the monastery of Sing

world's highest, barely a century before that, in 1852. Till then called Peak XV, the Survey's officers named it after a previous Surveyor General, Sir George Everest. Efforts to establish its exact altitude continued even after 1953, and the currently accepted height of 8848 metres was not finalised until 1958.

The first recorded efforts to scale Everest were launched from Tibet, up the north-eastern ridge. Between 1921 and 1938, seven such expeditions failed. After Nepal opened its

Trekkers in the snow: Everest Area.

Gompa. Then, heading north, following the Bhote Kosi river (the upper reaches of the Trisuli) to Syabrubensi. Turning east, along the gorge of Langtang Khola, the heavily forested trail eventually yields to extensive pasture lands that justify the cheese factory at Kyangjin Gompa (3540 metres).

Trekking and climbing activities in the country really took off after Hillary and Tenzing crested the Everest in May 1953. The Survey of India had recognised the peak as the

Himalayas to foreign climbers, three expeditions dug their crampons on the south east ridge, between 1951 and 1952.

By 1960, all of Nepal's 8000 metre high peaks had been climbed. Expeditions and climbers were looking for novel ways to achieve their 'firsts'. All the while expeditions grew more complex, the logistics remained truly military in scale. Then a school teacher from Austria, Reinhold Messner, set another record. In 1978, he and his partner Habeler climbed Everest without artificial oxygen. Later that year, he climbed Nanga Parbat alone, the first solo conquest of an 8000 metre peak. 'Loneliness', he said, 'is a force that can kill you if you are unprepared for it, but it will carry you beyond your own horizon if you understand how to use it to your advantage.' Two years later, this inner strength took him to the Everest again, where in four historic days, he climbed alone from the base camp to the peak and back again.

much more adventurous way of getting there, in this case, rafting down the Trisuli. The 'rafts' are really rubber dinghies, virtually unsinkable. They have been known to drop the unsuspecting into chilly water— once the initial shock has passed and the life vest has brought one to the surface, 'body surfing' is fun, feet pointing downstream, head looking straight up at unimaginably blue skies.

River running in the Himalayas began only in the 1970's, but today there is a wide choice

Yaks, the long-haired Asiatic oxen inhabit the upper reaches of the Khumbu valley.

The fastest way to the Everest and back again is however, a lot easier. Everyday (twice during the peak season) the 'Mountain Flight' that takes off from Kathmandu carries a plane load of passengers to within hailing distance of Nepal's highest peaks, including the Mount Everest. At the end of the flight, there's a certificate to boot!

Setting its sight much lower, another flight wings its way south, to the game reserve of Royal Chitwan. As always in Nepal, there is a

of rafting activities. The most popular are on the Sun Kosi, east of Kathmandu, where an encounter with the rapids can be a one -day picnic or a ten-day expedition. The most challenging are on the river Arun that drains the eastern Khumbu.

By the time these mountain streams descend to the flat green of the Terai, they become muddy. The moist lowlands through which they pass were once lush wooded jungles, natural stamping grounds for elephants and

tigers, rhinoceros and leopard, deer and wild boar. Chitwan in particular, was a favourite hunting ground of the Ranas. Under the onslaught of rapid twentieth century developments, the forests have dwindled with the twin attacks of the timber merchant's axe and the farmers plough. The continued survival of many species was called into question. In response, the late King Mahendra, declared the Royal Chitwan Park a rhinoceros preserve in 1962. Today some 200 great one-horned rhinos roam its 900 square kilometers of forest, and are often sighted from atop elephants out on safaris. The tourist is also likely to sight deer, buffalo, crocodile, monkeys and depending on the season, various species of birds. However, the star attraction is the Bengal tiger.

This border area of the Terai has traditionally been of peripheral interest to the western tourist. The creation of other wildlife reserves, Koshi Tappu in the east and the Royal Bardia in the west, should stimulate more traffic into this part of the country.

Indian travellers have often journeyed into the Terai, not just for trade but also on pilgrimage to Janakpur, the legendary capital of the ancient kingdom of Mithila. It is believed to be the birthplace of Sita, who married Rama, the hero of the Hindu epic *Ramayana*. Though no architectural evidence of the ancient city survives in Janakpur, pilgrims flock to the temple, (built eighty years ago) to celebrate Rama's birthday on *Ramnavami* in April every year.

At Lumbini, the acknowledged birthplace of Lord Buddha, a great deal of historical evidence survives. Close to the major border crossing at Sunauli, Lumbini is particularly famous for the pillar that Ashoka erected here in BC 250. Another hallowed place, believed to be the spot where Buddha was born, is the shrine of Maya Devi, Buddha's mother. *Chaityas* from the third century BC lend weight to the belief that Lumbini was Buddha's birthplace. But he may well have been born at Tilaurakot, 27 kilometres west of Lumbini, as

Facing page: Mustang, a remote desert region to the north of Nepal, it was formerly an autonomous Tibetan state, cut off from the outside world. It has since become a subject of the Nepal monarchy.

archaeologists have established the fact that it was the capital during his father's reign. Here, as always in Nepal, fact and legend are inseparable, intertwining enchanting skeins in the colourful threads of its romantic past.

VI

FOR ONE MONTH, the massive chariot grinds through the streets of Patan, pulled by soldiers of the Nepalese army. Its occupant is a red

An estimated 300 rhinoceros are resident in the Royal Chitwan Park's tall grassy swamplands.

wooden statue with slanting eyes flanked by large golden ears. Adorned with jewellery and decorated with flowers, Rato Macchendranath makes the slow journey to Jawlakhel, where on the last day of the festival, the King and Queen of Nepal seek his blessings. Like thousands of their subjects, they witness the display of the sacred *bhoto* (tunic), believed to have been given to Macchendranath for safe keeping by Karkot Naga, the snake god.

Many centuries ago, a king had sought the help of Macchendranath to end a twelve year dry spell in the valley. The legend says that the king's spiritual advisors attributed the drought to Gorakhnath, who had incarcerated the valley's rain gods. Only his guru, Macchendranath could persuade Gorakhnath to liberate them. Karkot Naga joined the expedition to Assam, the god's home in north-eastern India, and helped it overcome the supernatural impediments in its path. The party's first valley stop was at Bungamati, the site of the earlier Macchendranath temple, south of Patan. Gorakhnath trekked there to seek his guru's blessings, it is however not clear whether he received them or not. In any case, the imprisoned god wriggled free and the valley was blessed with rain.

Every year since then the valley's people have renewed their appeal to Macchendranath, now regarded as the god of rain and harvest. His permanent residence is a pagoda shaped temple, behind Patan's Durbar Square. It sits upon a platform with 108 prayer wheels, believed to correspond to the 108 forms of Avalokitesvara, the compassionate Buddha. Macchendranath, or the guarantor of rains, is the valley's most popular deity; Rato (red) in Patan, Seto (white) in Kathmandu, he is worshipped by both Buddhists and Hindus, who admit no conflict in their parallel faiths.

Historical accounts relating to the eighth century show that during the reign of King Vrikshadeva, Buddhists grew to acquire considerable power. They founded an order called Punya Vihar (near Pashupatinath), whose priests tossed the remnants of their evening meal at the feet of Pashupati, the holiest Hindu god in the valley. In the morning, they bathed the statue and paid obeisance to it, tasks normally reserved for Hindu priests of the Brahmin sect. In Hindu eyes, their behaviour was travesty; matters escalated and a clash ensued. The Hindus lost and were driven out from the temple. The leftovers continued to fill the shrine, till the great Hindu reformer

Facing page: A devotee prostrating with lit lamps on his body—an offering to Rato Macchendranath.

Sankaracharya arrived on the scene, to restore the temple to Hindus.

Nepalese Buddhists were now forced to look north towards Tibet. Their religious institutions never regained self-sufficiency and were supported either by Nepalese royalty, or, as in the case of Bodhnath, by Tibetan orders.

In a historical sense, Tibetan Buddhists were repaying a debt. The beginnings of the religion in their land did, after all, lie in Nepal, in the marriage of the Nepalese princess Bhrikuti to Tibetan King Tsrong-tsong Gompo. By the time this happened in the seventh century BC, Buddhism was already an ancient religion. The founder of the faith, Gautam Buddha, was born around BC 543 at Lumbini in Nepal's terai. But Buddhism came to Nepal much later, during the reign of the Indian emperor Ashoka, in the third century BC.

Gautam Siddhartha or Buddha, prince of the Sakya clan, was born of a miraculous conception. Astrologers predicted that he would either become a universal emperor or an enlightened being. To his father the choice was clear. He built a series of walls around the palace gardens, insulating the prince from exposure to old age, sickness or death, awareness of which was predicted to set him on the road to asceticism. Inevitably, reality intervened, and at the age of 29, the prince set forth to practise the austerities of monkhood. Enlightenment came after he realised the futility of these exercises—'a life of pleasure—this is low and ignoble, unworthy and useless and runs counter to the affairs of the spirit: and a life of fasting—this is sad, unworthy and useless'. In his first sermon at Sarnath, a deer park near the holy city of Benares, he advocated—'the middle way, which leads to repose, knowledge, illumination, *nirvana*. The origin of pain is thirst of pleasure, thirst of existence . . . Destroy your passions as the elephant would trample down a reed hut: but I would have you know that it is a mistake that one can escape from one's passions by taking shelter in hermitages. The only remedy against evil is healthy reality'.

In time, Buddha's followers inevitably created a religion around his lucid, earthy philosophy. And when the Third Buddhist

Council met at Pataliputra, now Patna, in BC 250, it decided that Buddhism would actively seek converts. Initially artists refrained from depicting the founder of this religion, substituting a tree to suggest his enlightenment, a horse for his renunciation of a princely life, or a sun wheel for the illuminating law he put into motion with his first sermon. Over time, he came to be depicted in the form with which we are familiar—with the urn a mark between the eyebrows, the *ushisha* (cranial protuberance), and the large ears, inevitably seated in a meditative posture.

For many years his followers worshiped only Gautam Buddha. They acknowledged though, that he had been preceded by five other Buddhas, by Vipasyin, Sikhin, Visvabhu, Krakuchanda and Kashyapa. In time, an eighth Buddha would take human form—Maitreya, already a seeker of enlightenment *(bodhi),* or *Boddhisattvas* .

Around the first century BC, the *Boddhisattva* concept began to expand. Accumulating merit in birth after birth, the *Boddhisattvas* underlined the importance of good deeds, and held out the promise of salvation for greater numbers. They also represented a departure from orthodox Buddhism and prompted a major schism, formalised at the Fourth Buddhist Council held at Kashmir, in the second century AD. The *Mahayana* (greater vehicle), sect born of this divide, spread to the north and east. Influenced by the earlier Bon religion, in Tibet it took a unique form that influenced religious developments in Nepal.

A major feature of Tibetan Buddhism is its belief in reincarnation. Its spiritual authority, the Dalai Lama, is regarded as the reincarnation of his predecessor and is identified while still a child. Echoed at different levels by other *Rimpoche* (reincarnate lamas), the search for the Dalai Lama is guided by supernatural indications, including the ability of the child to recognise possessions from an earlier life. (Interestingly, this test is shared by the would be Kumari, the living goddess in Kathmandu.)

At the visible level, the iconography of Buddhism in Nepal is obviously influenced by the Hindu religion. The splendid gilded *vajra,* or symbolic thunderbolt that stands at the head of the Swayambunath stairs is speculated to be a throwback of the thunderbolt of Indra, ancient Hindu god of fire. A mythological detective would find it fruitful to explore this connection via the bearer of the thunderbolt, Bodhisattva Vajrapani. Like the Avalokitesvara, Vajrapani was born of the *dhyan* (meditation) of one of the *dhvani* Buddhas, in this case Akshobhya. Like the Hindu gods, each of the *dhyani* Buddhas is associated with a ritual mount. For both Vajrapani and Indra, the trusted *vahana* (vehicle), is the elephant!

Statues of the *dhyani* Buddhas are common to most Nepali *stupas,* each in a prescribed *asana* (posture), hands arranged in a *mudra* (formalised gesture). At the centre is Vairochana, in the north Amoghasiddhi, Akshobhya faces east, Ratnasambhava south, guarding the west is Amitabha with his peacock mount and the lotus flower that was passed on to Bodhisattva Avalokitesvara. It is this lotus flower that is the object of the chant, *Om Mani Padme Hum,* (Oh! jewel in the lotus), the prayer with which the Tibetan Buddhist places himself in the benign care of the Avalokitesvara.

Attributes such as the lotus have long been associated with iconic forms of the gods—Zeus too had a thunderbolt, Pan a flute, Cupid his bow and arrow. But in the Hindu pantheon, an elaborate code of association was essential to the identity of gods. A manual of identification would have to be cross-indexed not just by attribute and posture, gesture and mount, but for completeness also by colour, number of limbs and number of heads.

Nepalese kings are considered incarnations of Lord Vishnu. Orthodox Hindu tradition more conservatively restricts the 'preserver's' incarnations to ten, each earthly manifestation necessitated by conditions requiring divine intervention. In the first *avataar* (incarnation), Vishnu took the form of a fish and saved Manu, the progenitor of the human race, from the great deluge. In the second, as a tortoise

Facing page: *Monks from the 'Yellow Hats' sect of Buddhists participate in the Mani Rimdu festival. Dalai Lama, the most revered Buddhist religious authority also belongs to this sect.*

he lent his broad back to the gods churning *amrita*, the fluid of life. In the third, as a gigantic boar he rescued the earth from the clutches of the demon, Hiranyaaksha. In the fourth a man-lion, in the fifth a dwarf, it was in the sixth *avtaar* that Vishnu took human form. As Parasuram, he came to combat the hegemony of the *Kshatriya* caste, whose armies killed his father, Jamadagni. A Brahmin, Jamadagni is thought to represent the knowledge of god and Parasuram's retaliatory massacre of *Kshatriya* armies to symbolise divine concern with the well-being of the Brahmin caste.

VII

THE MOST CELEBRATED of Vishnu's avatars are the seventh and the eighth—Rama, hero of the epic *Ramayana,* and Krishna, enshrined both in the delightful verse of the Gita *Govinda* and in the loftier philosophy of the *Bhagavad* Gita, contained in the *Mahabharata. Holi,* the colourful festival held in spring, is thought to have its roots in Krishna's frolics.

Correspondingly, *Dasain,* Nepal's most lavishly celebrated festival, is traced back to the epic of *Ramayana*—to the victory of Lord Rama over his arch rival, the demon Ravana. Throughout the subcontinent, the *Ramayana* is a live epic, extensively staged, retold and read. Quite apart from the development of its plot, the religious virtue of *Ramayana* lies in its depiction of Rama, as the ideal man, whose virtue cannot be sullied, irrespective of the trials to which he is subjected. Throughout the tribulations in the epic, one of Rama's steadfast friends was Hanuman, the monkey god. It is to this role that he owes his extensive popularity.

In between *avtaars*, Vishnu is typically pictured as Narayana, floating on the cosmic ocean. The snake on which he lies is Ananta, literally without end, representing the infinity of time. It is in this form that he is viewed by the thousands who look upon the sixth century

Facing page: The sixth century image of Vishnu at Budhani Kantha. He is portrayed here as Narayana floating on the cosmic ocean, lying on Ananta, the snake.

image at Budhanilkantha. One person who will never be able to admire this five metre work of art is the King of Nepal, restrained by a superstition that to look upon it would invite death.

Death, of course is the domain of Shiva, considered in Nepal to be the most powerful of the Hindu triad. However, it is not this aspect of Shiva that draws hundreds of thousands to the Pashupatinath temple every year. Here, and indeed, in most Shiva shrines he is worshipped as 'creator', symbolised by a *lingam*—the most abstract of votive forms in a milieu which has spawned so much exquisite anthropomorphic art. Implicit in the Pashupatinath complex is another image of Shiva—chest garlanded with a string of skulls, signifying his role as 'destroyer'.

As destroyer and creator, Shiva is also thought to govern the rhythm of existence, the cosmic dance of the universe. Nataraja or the king of dance, he is Nasal, the god who occasioned the Nasal Chowk at the heart of Kathmandu. In this fearsome aspect, he is most often refered to as Bhairava, with protruding fangs and a severed head in his arms.

The severed head is also a distinguishing feature of the presiding deity at the valley's Dakshinakali temple—Ma Kali, black mother, or Mahakali. Hindu myth reveres her as the wife of Shiva. Her importance as mother goddess flows from the belief that greatest gods can have no direct contact with the mortal world. The responsibility for this contact belongs to their emanations, their *shakti,* or divine power, normally represented as wife or daughter. As Nataraja dances the rhythm of the cosmos, Kali dances the cycle of life. The severed heads represent both death and the extinction of human frailties. Also known as Durga, Kali is said to have developed a taste for blood when she killed the demon Raktavira. Brahma had bestowed upon his blood the ability to spawn a thousand clones for every drop that fell on the ground. To ensure his extinction, Kali was forced to pierce him with a spear and drink his blood straight from the wound.

Like her, imbued by philosophy, mythology, and centuries of animal sacrifice, are the other mother goddesses, the Ashtamatrikas, who exercise a deep influence over religious practise in Nepal .

Her festival, the ten day *Durga Puja,* or *Dasain,* parallels the *Dussebra* celebrations that feature Lord Rama. As they commemorate his victory over Ravana, they also pay homage to the divine mother for slaying the thousand-headed monster who threatened the universe. For nine nights, masked performers dance in the streets of Patan, possessed, it seems, by an unearthly energy. On the seventh day,

swift blow of the sacrificial blade. Through the night the rites continue, culminating at dawn in public sacrifices at the square outside Kathmandu's Hanuman Dhoka.

The blood so split is holy, its *tilak,* or mark, an auspicious sign that decorates cars and buses, shovels and ploughs; warding off evil, attracting success. Magnanimous after the wholehearted propitiation, this one day the deity of the Taleju temple opens her doors to the thronging devotees.

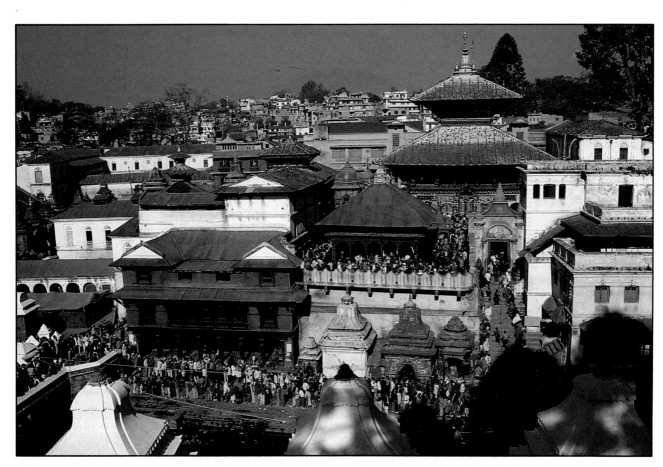

The Pashupatinath temple, among the holiest of Hindu shrines, during the Teej *festival.*

manifestations of monarchical splendour compete for attention—cannons boom at the Tundikhel parade grounds, while the King and Queen review their troops.

The next day, the devout fast in ritual preparation for *kal ratri* (the dark night), that belongs entirely to Durga. Black buffaloes fill in for the demon she slaughtered, their sacrificial blood mixing with the blood of chickens and goats, sheep and ducks, their cowering earthly misery terminated with one

Vijay Dasami, the tenth day of the moon, marks the victory (*vijay*) of Rama and Durga. Hindus receive *tika*—this time a dab of vermillion powder—from their elders, a lucky few from the King and Queen, who parade through Kathmandu's Durbar Street.

October-November is the festival season in

Facing page: *Masked dancers of Nepal. Believed to be possessed by spirits, many still perform in a tradition of story-telling.*

70

Nepal. Three weeks after *Dasain* is *Tihar,* the counterpart of the Indian festival of *Diwali.* This festival of lights too, is believed to have its origins in the *Ramayana,* and marks the victorious return of Rama from his expedition to Ravana's island kingdom. On the first day, rice, meat or specially prepared delicacies are fed to crows, the messengers of King Yama, the lord of death. On the second, floral honours are heaped on dogs, who are believed to guide souls across the river of death. The third day belongs to Lakshmi, the goddess of wealth, associated with the cows who are also worshipped on this day. It is also believed that she will leave the skies moonless, for homes that are illuminated on this evening. Through the night, the oil lamps twinkle on every window sill, freshly painted shutters are left open to welcome the generosity of her blessings.

The fourth day of *Tihar* coincides with the Newari New Year, and is the day for the worship of bulls. On the fifth and last day, the second day of the new moon, sisters ask their brothers to renew their pledge of lifelong protection, which males today symbolise with gifts of money or clothes.

The first major festival of the Newari Year, the last if one follows the Gregorian calendar, is *Balachaturdashi,* a ritualised memorial service for the well being of ancestors. Appropriately, the main activity is in the area where their mortal remains are consigned to the gods, near Pashupatinath, particularly around the Mrigasthali hill, considered the residence of countless deities. Those who observe the festival, take a ritual walk around the hill. Visiting its shrines, they feed the monkeys, a virtuous act that is supposed to directly benefit the dead in their family.

By now it is typically early December and the festival calendar takes a break for the Himalayan winter. But not for long. By late February or early March, it is time to celebrate *Shivaratri,* the night of Lord Shiva. At Pashupatinath, pilgrims crowd the Bagmati ghats, constructed like those at Benares. Already purified by day long fasts, devotees cleanse themselves in the cold waters. Till the cold dawn, votive lamps flicker on the banks,

or float gently downstream. In little clusters, or larger groups, drums pound and devotees sing in praise of the lord. In his domain, the King orders a volley of gunfire to honour the powerful lord, also known as the patron of the ascetics. Smeared with dust and ashes, their hair arranged in matted coils, the *sadhus* wander into the valley, practising their austerities, or smoking the clay pipes of *charas* that have been their privilege since their lord set the example.

Even before its really warm enough for water frolics, the festival calendar serves up *Holi,* the festival of colour, dedicated to Krishna and through him to Vishnu. The young take the festival to the streets, faces painted with garish colours, their water-filled balloons and pails of coloured water legitimate ammunition against any passer-by, the more familiar the better.

Marking the Nepalese New Year, at the beginning of the Hindu month of *Baisakha,* is the *Bisket* festival. Observed throughout the valley, *Bisket* is most exciting at Bhaktapur. Appropriately so, for it is here that legend sets the origins of this festival: one of the kings of this ancient city had a daughter who was, it seems, a female Blackbeard. Every night, a young man was recruited to satisfy her passions; every morning, his corpse was carried out, till a foreign prince volunteered to switch places with the local talent. That night, the princess slept sated. The hero of our legend kept watch over her chamber and saw twin serpents grow out of her nostrils, searching for their nightly victim. The princess' fate is unknown, but the snakes were, obviously, put to death, their carcasses hung from a pole in the city square for the benefit of the rejoicing young men, now delivered from the hands of death. On the day before the New Year, an eighty foot pole is erected in Bhaktapur, recalling this victory and the snakes of the legend now replaced by long sweeping banners.

The two other major festivals during the first month of the Nepalese year are Buddhist in origin—the all important *Macchendranath Yatra* at Patan, and *Buddha Jay anti.* Observed in every Buddhist home and shrine, but most spectacularly at Swayambunath, the celebrations for Buddha's birthday coincide with the anniversary of his enlightenment and of his departure from earth. On the full moon night in April/May, butter lamps light the niches of the Swayambunath *stupa*. Lay folk stream up the stairs to the hilltop decorated with flowers, prayer flags and *tangkhas,* where burgundy swathed monks perform the prescribed rituals. At Bodhnath, lamas proceed in the wake of an elephant carrying an image of the Buddha.

and are not punctuated by any festivals, which resume their annual cycle in the month of *Shravan,* the monsoon month of July/August. On the day of Ghantakarna's procession, crosses and arches of bamboo, straw or wooden branches stand in for the demon Ghantakarna, and are erected at crossroads, thought to be the common haunts of witches and demons. Along with the effigies, urchins position themselves so as to extract contributions towards the funeral of

A local woman displaying a myriad of colours on the occasion of Holi, *the festival of colours dedicated to Lord Krishna, when the young take to the streets, their faces painted and their pails full of coloured water.*

Around the shrine, the elephant leads the growing stream of followers, through the streets to Chabahil, where Emperor Ashoka's daughter Charumati is said to have built the *stupa*. Watched by its four pairs of eyes, they pay homage to the princess who is believed to have sponsored the spread of Buddhism in their country.

The succeeding months of *Jyestha* and *Ashada* are generally considered inauspicious

Ghantakarna, (Bell Ears), who they claim left his wives without any money. Throughout the day, additions are made to the representation of the demon—evil face masks, pumpkins painted with sexual organs and miniature demon puppets.

Then, in the evening, a human masquerader of Ghantakarna makes his way through the crowds that surround the effigy. His arrival is the signal to set flaming torches to it. Down to

the river the victorious crowds proceed, dragging the smoking effigies with them whose ashes are cast into the water.

Two other major festivals are also occasions for processions—*Gaijatra,* the procession of cows in the month of *Bhadra,* and *Indrajatra,* in the succeeding month of *Asvina* (Septempber/October).

The masked youth and cows that parade through the valley's cities represent those dead since the last *Gaijatra.* But the procession is far

tradition of glasnost, the closeted treasures of temples are brought into public view— statues and reliquaries, normally seen only by their guardians.

Indrajatra, literally the procession of Lord Indra, actually recalls the search for him by his mount. Taken for a common criminal, the supreme lord was held in Kathmandu, while his elephant searched the streets for him. The first day of the festival depicts the joy of the elephant when Indra's mother came down from

In the folk tradition of Nepal, a group of Nepali men playing the flute to the beat of the drum—old tunes which have been handed down from generation to generation.

from mournful, its object to remind the mourners that they are not alone. The tradition began as an attempt by a king to console his queen, distraught at the death of their son. In the afternoon, troupes perform traditional dances at public squares. Flowing from the same king's efforts to entertain his wife, the festival observes a lasting tradition of caricature and social and political satire, maintained even through the days of repression. In the same

the heavens to arrange the release of her son. Recognising that this demonstration of happiness is beyond the abilities of the ordinary elephant, today's procession makes

Facing page: *Bhaktapur women and children during a festival.*
Following pages 76-77: *Almost every month is a festival month in Nepal, each being an occasion for national celebration.*

believe with a masked dancer, illuminated by torchlight. The high point of the festivities is actually the procession of another deity, the living goddess, her chariot flanked by dancers depicting Ganesh and Bhairava. Bhairava is the other god honoured during the *Indrajatra* . His awesome gold mask, normally covered, is exposed for the occasion and rice beer allowed to issue from his mouth. Crowds wrestle for the privilege of drinking the beer, blessed by the mighty Bhairava. At some point, a live fish

region, suffered from the official antipathy towards artistic expression in the pre-1951 era. Today, patronage is surfacing, but revival of these fragile art forms is a slow and demanding process.

The best preserved dances are those staged in the Buddhist monasteries, in their courtyards or *cham-ras* . The very word *cham* means dance, and probably comes from Shamanism, the ritual that drives out evil spirits and appeases guardian spirits with human and

In Nepal, obedience to religious laws and placation through rituals are part of everyday life—men bearing oil lamps, diyas *on their body.*

passes through his mouth—its recipient considered the most blessed of all.

Prancing through festive streets, many of Nepal's masked dancers are believed to be possessed by spirits. Still others perform in a tradition of storytelling, recounting ancient stories of good and evil. Every region has its folk dances brought to the valley for major festivals. But the classical dances, influenced by the various schools of dance in the South Asian

animal sacrifice. When the Indian teacher Padmasambhava helped spread Buddhism in Tibet in the eighth century AD, he saw in this accepted dance drama an opportunity to further his own objectives. He adapted the Shamanistic dance, ridding it of the blood sacrifices abhorrent to his own faith, replacing them with effigies and red coloured substances. The yak that was customarily sacrificed before the dance, is still put through its ritual cleansing, but then released to wander in the Himalayas—the holy mountains invoked to bless the dance. The very interpretation of the dance was altered, and under the new dispensation, taken to represent the triumph of Buddhism over Shamanism.

Now, when the first dancers emerge into the *cham-ras,* their black wide-brimmed hats topped with simulated skulls, are said to represent the disguise worn by Dpal-gyi-rdo-je, a ninth century Tibetan monk who assassinated

monastery orchestra is said to correspond to a sound inherent in the human body. Otherwise accessible only by meditation, their tones and the liturgical chants that accompany them have a brooding quality, justifying the claim that they are aids to contemplation and prayer.

In the folk tradition of lower Nepal, wandering minstrels once played the *sarangi,* the bow-stringed instrument common to Indian folk and classical music. The songs they sang in village clearings were often ballads, new

Masked youth and cows prance through the valley's festive streets in a procession, representing those dead since the last Gaijatra.

the anti-Buddhist King Glag-dar-ma. Earlier representing various spirits, the masks are now visages of Buddhist deities, the most impressive of whom is Chos-kyi-rgyal-po. His handsome bullhead is emblematic of the deity that vanquishes the god of the dead.

Accompanying the *cham* are the prolonged deep sounds, bass chants and sharp rhythms of Tibetan music, easily accessible at Bodhnath on festival days. Every instrument of the

stories set to old tunes, or religious songs handed down from generation to generation. Today, the village audiences that hear them are crouched in front of transistor radios. Today's troubadours cater largely to urban audiences and to the studios of Radio Nepal.

Following page 80: *Portrait of a* Gurung *woman, a people who inhabit the Marsyangali valley near Annapurna.*